ALLIGATOR

ALLIGATOR

by Evelyn Shaw

Pictures by Frances Zweifel

SCHOLASTIC BOOK SERVICES
NEW YORK · TORONTO · LONDON · AUCKLAND · SYDNEY · TOKYO

Text copyright © 1972 by Evelyn Shaw. Pictures copyright © 1972 by Frances W. Zweifel. All rights reserved. This edition is published by Scholastic Book Services, a division of Scholastic Magazines, Inc., 50 West 44th Street, New York, N.Y. 10036, by arrangement with Harper & Row, Publishers, Inc.

12 11 10 9 8 7 6 5 4 3 2 1   4   9/7 0 1 2 3 4/8

Printed in the U.S.A.   07

To Anne, Judith, David, and Matthew

and

Matthew, Kenneth, and Ellen

The morning mist hides the swamp.

It hides the trees and plants.

It hides the resting animals.

The morning light grows brighter.

Animals begin to move.

10

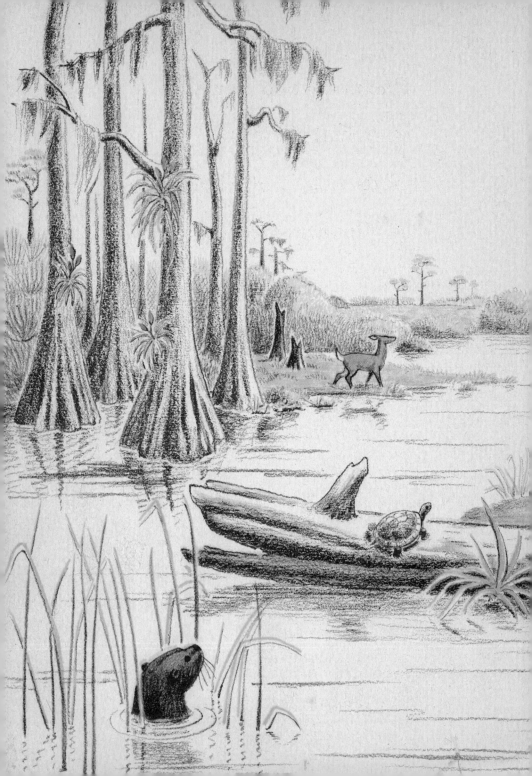

Raccoons and bears
stretch their legs.
Birds raise their heads
and look around.

An alligator sits

on a mat of grass

near the creek.

14

The alligator is ten feet long.

It is so big that it is safe

from all other animals.

The alligator begins to move.

It is a female.

About one month before, she mated

with a male alligator.

Now the time has come

for her to lay her eggs.

She has to make a big nest

for the eggs.

She works on her nest

for several days.

She stomps on the grass

to make it flat.

She tears twigs and leaves

from small trees

with her huge mouth.

She pulls them onto the flat grass.

She tears up reeds

and drags them to her nest.

She dives into the water

and pulls up water plants.

The plants have mud

on their roots.

The alligator puts them

on her nest.

The nest grows higher and higher.

It is a thick wet mound

of plants and twigs and mud.

It is almost two feet high.

The alligator lays

forty eggs in the nest.

She covers the eggs

with more plants and mud.

The mud and plants

hide the eggs.

The eggs cannot be seen.

But some animals

can dig them out of the nest.

Raccoons and bears

eat alligator eggs.

One bear can eat all forty of them.

So the mother alligator

stays close to her nest

most of the time.

But sometimes she has to leave it.

She has to find fish or turtles

to eat.

One morning the alligator

is away from her nest.

She is looking for food.

A raccoon comes through the plants near the nest.
It is looking for food too.

The raccoon sees

the alligator's nest.

It starts digging

into the mound to get the eggs.

Suddenly, the mother alligator

raises her huge head

out of the water.

She snorts and makes

loud hissing noises.

She rushes toward the nest.

The raccoon runs away

as fast as it can.

The summer passes.

The mother alligator

has been guarding her eggs

for two months.

One night in late August,

she is resting

near the nest.

33

Suddenly, she hears

a strange noise.

Two men are rowing a boat

on the creek.

They are hunters

looking for alligators.

They want to shoot an alligator.

They want to sell its skin.

The mother alligator

sits very still.

One hunter fires his gun at her.

The bullet hits the top of her back,

but she is not hurt.

She folds her short thick legs

against her body.

She swishes her powerful tail.

She dives into the creek

and disappears under the water.

Farther down the creek

she comes up again.

She stays so still

that she looks like a floating log.

Later she tries

to go back to her nest.

The hunters are still there.

She has to stay away from her nest.

Inside the nest,

the baby alligators begin to hatch.

More and more babies

come out of their eggshells.

But they cannot

get out of the nest.

They cannot get through the plants
that cover them.
If they do not get out soon,
they will die.
After they leave the eggshells,
they need air and food.

The mother alligator

has to uncover them.

But she cannot

get back to the nest.

Then the hunters see

another alligator

climb out of the water.

It is even bigger than the mother.

They row over to it.

One of the men fires a shot at it,
but he does not hit it.
The alligator gives a loud roar.
It goes after the boat.

One hunter is knocked down
in the boat.

The other hunter

rows the boat away

as fast as he can.

Now it is safe

for the mother alligator

to come back to her nest.

She climbs out of the water

and rests near it.

She hears the baby alligators

making soft sounds

inside the nest.

She clears away

part of the nest.

49

Forty wriggling baby alligators

come out of their dark nest

into the morning light.

They look like their mother.

But they are only nine inches long.

They scamper over to her.

She makes soft grunting noises.

They stay together.

A few days later the mother

dives into the water

to look for food.

She sees something dark

coming toward her.

She becomes very quiet.

The dark thing is a school of fish.

There are hundreds of fish

in the school.

They come closer and closer.

With a swish of her thick tail,

the mother tosses some fish

onto the bank.

She climbs out of the water

and begins chewing the fish.

Her babies eat

the small pieces of fish

that fall out of her mouth.

Soon the babies begin hunting

for their own food.

They grow larger.

When winter comes,

they rest in dens.

In the spring

each young alligator

finds its own place to live.

In about ten years,

if they are not killed

by other animals or hunters,

the alligators will be

as big as their mother.

They will be

one of the many kinds of animals

that live in the southern swamp.

60

AUTHOR'S NOTE

The alligator in this book is *Alligator mississippiensis*. It lives in the southeastern part of the United States.

A naturalist named E. A. McIlhenny watched this kind of alligator in the wild for many years. In 1935 he published a book about them. His book is called *The Alligator's Life History*. Most of the facts we know about these alligators come from Mr. McIlhenny's book.

Since then, people have hunted and killed many alligators. People have drained many of the swamps in which alligators used to live. As a result of these pressures, some alligators may have changed their ways of life.